WE'RE ALL WORKS OF ART

For Rubin – M.S.

For Mabel Trivett and Art Rowlands... both works of art – R.B.

First published in the UK in 2018 by
Pavilion Books Company Limited
43 Great Ormond Street
London
WC1N 3HZ

Text © Mark Sperring, 2018
Illustrations © Rose Blake, 2018
'We're all styles of art' text written by Mandy Archer, © Pavilion Books Company Limited, 2018

The moral rights of the author and illustrator have been asserted

Publisher and Editor: Neil Dunnicliffe
Assistant Editor: Harriet Grylls
Art Director: Anna Lubecka

ISBN: 9781843653486

A CIP catalogue record for this book is available from the British Library.

10 9 8 7 6 5 4 3 2 1

Reproduction by Mission, Hong Kong
Printed by Toppan Leefung, Ltd China

This book can be ordered directly from the publisher online at www.pavilionbooks.com,
or try your local bookshop.

WE'RE ALL WORKS OF ART

WRITTEN BY
Mark Sperring

ILLUSTRATED BY
Rose Blake

PAVILION

Our faces might seem angular,

with noses all askew.

Our skin tones might all vary,
we're every shade and hue.

Some people think we look surreal,

and frankly, yes, we do!

But we can make you tilt your head,

and see the
world anew.

Our feet might be so heavy
they root us to the floor,

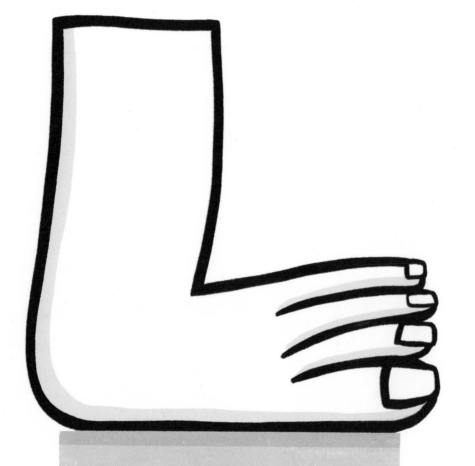

but we have a certain presence
that no one can ignore.

We might look rather classic,

or something else, less so.

or like no one
else you know.

We might look
quite familiar,

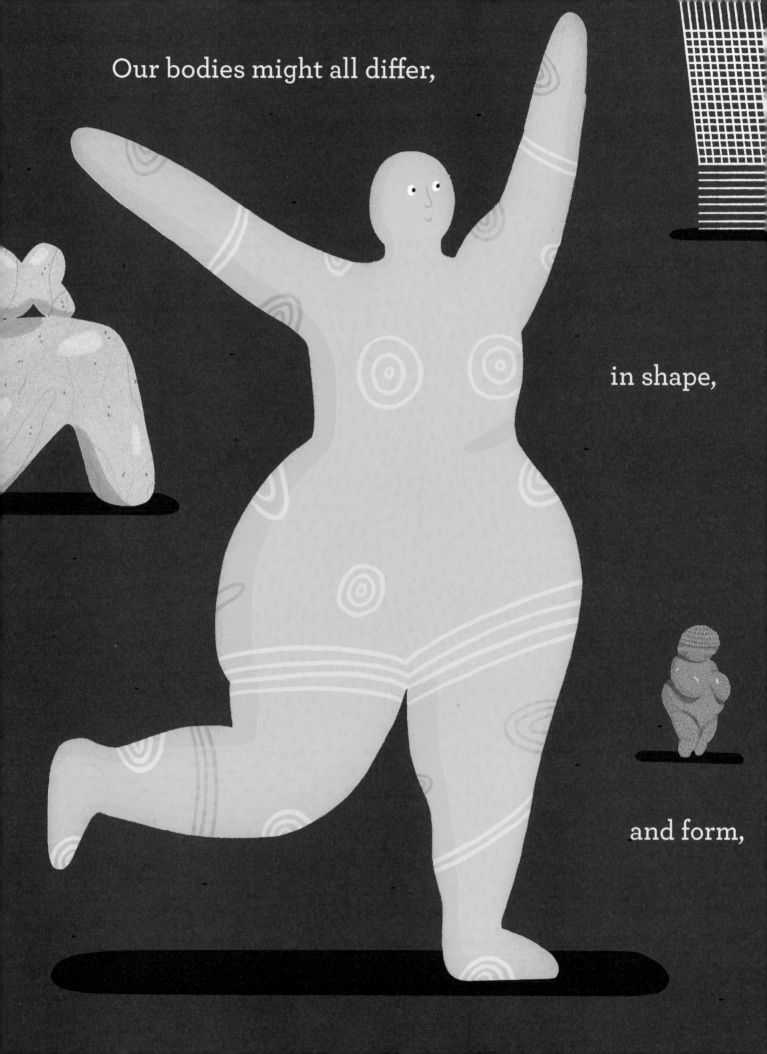

Our bodies might all differ,

in shape,

and form,

and frame...

...but think how dull the world would be

if we were all the same.

We might
look like
a collage,

made up from this and that...

...but we wouldn't change
a mis-matched ear,

or swap one
single scrap.

Whoever it was that made us,

made us each with loving care.

Each curve and kink and scribbly line

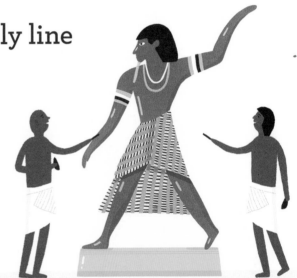

was meant to be right there.

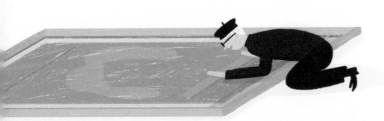

We are proud of our uniqueness,
and deep down in our hearts

we know we are
spectacular...

...for we're all works of art!

WE'RE ALL STYLES OF ART

This book features all sorts of spectacular styles of painting, collage and sculpture.

These pages introduce you to some of the art styles that appear in this book, but this is just the start! Impressionism, Bauhaus, art nouveau – there are so many more amazing movements and artists to find out about. You can explore books, go online or visit galleries.

Prehistoric art

For thousands of years, people have been making pictures, arranging stones and carving shapes out of bone. The first humans ground burned wood, animal fat and soil into paint, then daubed shapes and symbols on their cave walls. Their prehistoric works of art have meaning and tell stories that we may never fully understand.

Explore → the El Castillo cave paintings • Stonehenge • Aboriginal rock art • Paleolithic Venus figurines •

Egyptian art

Between 2,000 and 5,000 years ago, Egypt was at the heart of a very powerful civilization. Over this time, Ancient Egyptian art changed very little. The most respected artists copied the style of their ancestors. Nearly all Egyptian art focused on the afterlife. Temples and tombs were filled with paintings to honour the mighty Pharaohs – the rulers of the land.

Explore → the Great Pyramids • the gold mask of Tutankhamun • the bust of Nefertiti •

Greek art

The Ancient Greeks decorated their buildings, homes and streets with art. They were skilled at making beautiful pottery, intricate mosaic floors and lavish wall paintings. Many Ancient Greek sculptures were carved out of marble – a hard, glossy stone that can survive for thousands of years. They featured almost perfect poses of Greek gods and mythical heroes from the past.

Explore → the Parthenon • Phidias • Apelles of Kos •

Indian miniatures

Indian art has a long and varied tradition that crosses many forms, ages and societies. Its rich heritage includes sculpture, jewellery, textiles and stunning miniatures. Indian miniatures are small-scale paintings known for their vivid colours and breathtaking brushwork. These mini masterpieces were created on palm leaves and then, later, paper.

Explore ➡ the great schools of miniature painting – including Pala, Jain and Mughal •

Renaissance art

During the 1500s, painters and sculptors began to look back to the myths, legends and symbols of the Ancient world. They created works of art in a classical style, paying great attention to the detail and realism in their work. The Renaissance era in Europe is often described as the 'golden' age of art. Some of the world's most famous artists are from this time.

Explore ➡ Titian • Michelangelo • Leonardo da Vinci • Marcus Gheeraerts the Younger •

Fauvism

The Fauvists were a small group of artists that worked during the early 20th century. The name for the art movement comes from the word les fauves, which means 'the wild beasts'. Fauvists used strong colours to reveal their moods and ideas. This gave artists the freedom to express themselves without having to create realistic images of the world that they saw in front of them.

Explore ➡ André Derain • Raoul Dufy • Henri Matisse •

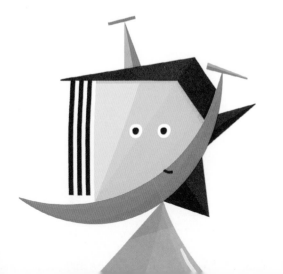

Cubism

Pablo Picasso and the Cubists shook up the art world when their movement started to emerge! They looked at images in a completely different way – breaking their subjects down into a combination of flat, geometric shapes. Cubists were also fascinated by perspective. They often tried to paint things from a number of different angles within the same piece.

Explore ➡ Pablo Picasso • Georges Braque • Fernand Léger •

Surrealism

The Surrealists weren't just artists, their movement influenced books and philosophy, too. Paintings in this style were inspired by dreams, so they often featured strange and impossible situations. Well-known Surrealist masterpieces include work by René Magritte, who painted floating cats in hats, and Salvador Dalí, who imagined a slippery, dripping clock!

Explore ➡ Salvador Dalí · René Magritte · Lee Miller · Joan Miró ·

Pop art

Pop art, or 'popular art' exploded in the USA and Europe during the 1950s and '60s. It combined bright colours with ideas from comic books, pop music, celebrities and advertising. The young artists of the time tried to push back against old-fashioned, traditional views on art and painting. Their work was bold, bright and super-modern.

Explore ➡ Andy Warhol · Peter Blake · Roy Lichtenstein · Pauline Boty · Jean-Michel Basquiat ·

Contemporary art

'Contemporary' is a way of describing the work created by artists who are alive today and those of our recent past. It includes all sorts of amazing art styles – from eye-popping abstract works to more realistic paintings, installations and sculptures. Contemporary art can be inspired by anything in our modern society, from the latest technology to time and memory. It is innovative, original and exciting.

Explore ➡ David Shrigley · Rachel Whiteread · Antony Gormley · Ai Weiwei · Steve McQueen ·

What about you?

Do you like being creative? Perhaps the great artists have inspired you to paint a picture or mould a shape out of modelling clay? Making – and enjoying – art has no limits. Art can be anything that you want it to be. Give it a go. Make your own unique masterpiece today!